Flower Colours

Written by Josephine Selwyn

Picture Dictionary

blue

orange

pink

Read the picture dictionary. You will find these words in the book.

red

white

yellow

Here is a flower.

red

Here is a flower.

yellow

Here is a flower.

blue

Here is a flower.

white

Here is a flower.

pink

Here is a flower.

orange

Activity Page

Make flower puzzles.

1. Cut out photos of flowers from magazines.
2. Glue the photos onto cardboard.
3. Cut into two or three pieces for a puzzle.

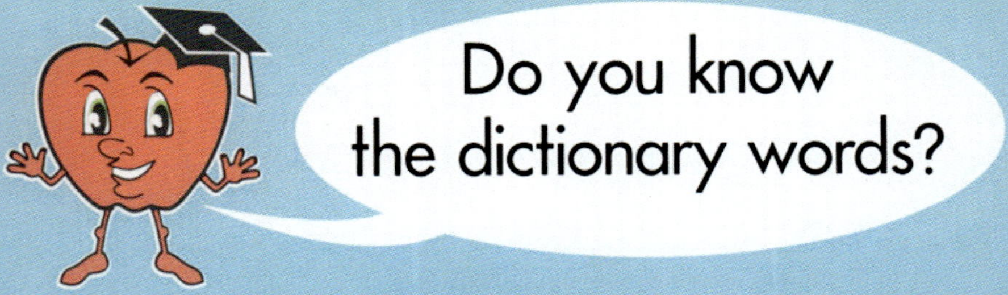